Earth's Record Breakers

By NADIA HIGGINS

Illustrations by JIA LIU

Music by MARK OBLINGER

CANTATA
LEARNING

WWW.CANTATALEARNING.COM

CANTATA LEARNING

Published by Cantata Learning
1710 Roe Crest Drive
North Mankato, MN 56003
www.cantatalearning.com

Library of Congress Cataloging-in-Publication Data
Names: Higgins, Nadia, author. | Liu, Jia (Illustrator), illustrator. |
   Oblinger, Mark, composer.
Title: Earth's record breakers / by Nadia Higgins ; illustrated by Jia Liu ;
   music by Mark Oblinger.
Description: North Mankato, MN : Cantata Learning, [2018] | Series: What
   shapes our Earth? | Includes lyrics and sheet music. | Audience: Ages 6–9.
   | Audience: K to grade 3. | Includes bibliographical references.
Identifiers: LCCN 2017017528 (print) | LCCN 2017036117 (ebook) | ISBN
   9781684101559 (ebook) | ISBN 9781684101351 (hardcover : alk. paper)
Subjects: LCSH: Earth (Planet)--Miscellanea--Juvenile literature. |
   Children's songs, English.
Classification: LCC QB631.4 (ebook) | LCC QB631.4 .H5394 2018 (print) | DDC
   525--dc23
LC record available at https://lccn.loc.gov/2017017528

Book design and art direction, Tim Palin Creative
Editorial direction, Kellie M. Hultgren
Music direction, Elizabeth Draper
Music arranged and produced by Mark Oblinger

Printed in the United States of America in North Mankato, Minnesota.
122017   0378CGS18

ACCESS THE MUSIC!
SCAN CODE WITH MOBILE APP
CANTATALEARNING.COM

TIPS TO SUPPORT LITERACY AT HOME

WHY READING AND SINGING WITH YOUR CHILD IS SO IMPORTANT

Daily reading with your child leads to increased academic achievement. Music and songs, specifically rhyming songs, are a fun and easy way to build early literacy and language development. Music skills correlate significantly with both phonological awareness and reading development. Singing helps build vocabulary and speech development. And reading and appreciating music together is a wonderful way to strengthen your relationship.

READ AND SING EVERY DAY!

TIPS FOR USING CANTATA LEARNING BOOKS AND SONGS DURING YOUR DAILY STORY TIME

1. As you sing and read, point out the different words on the page that rhyme. Suggest other words that rhyme.

2. Memorize simple rhymes such as Itsy Bitsy Spider and sing them together. This encourages comprehension skills and early literacy skills.

3. Use the questions in the back of each book to guide your singing and storytelling.

4. Read the included sheet music with your child while you listen to the song. How do the music notes correlate to the words of the song?

5. Sing along on the go and at home. Access music by scanning the QR code on each Cantata book. You can also stream or download the music for free to your computer, smartphone, or mobile device.

Devoting time to daily reading shows that you are available for your child. Together, you are building language, literacy, and listening skills.

Have fun reading and singing!

Our planet offers a world of wonders. Some of them are truly **extreme**. They have gone down in the record books. What is the highest mountain? Which river is the longest? Where is the world's most active volcano?

Turn the page. Sing along to this record-breaking song!

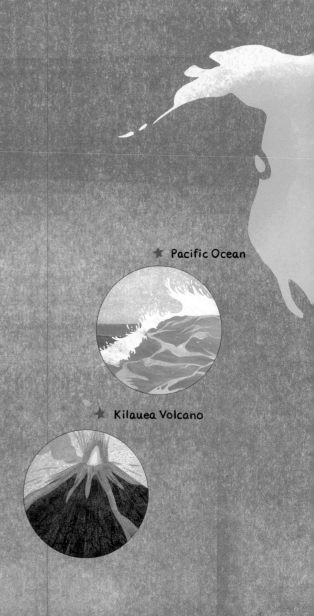

Pacific Ocean

Kilauea Volcano

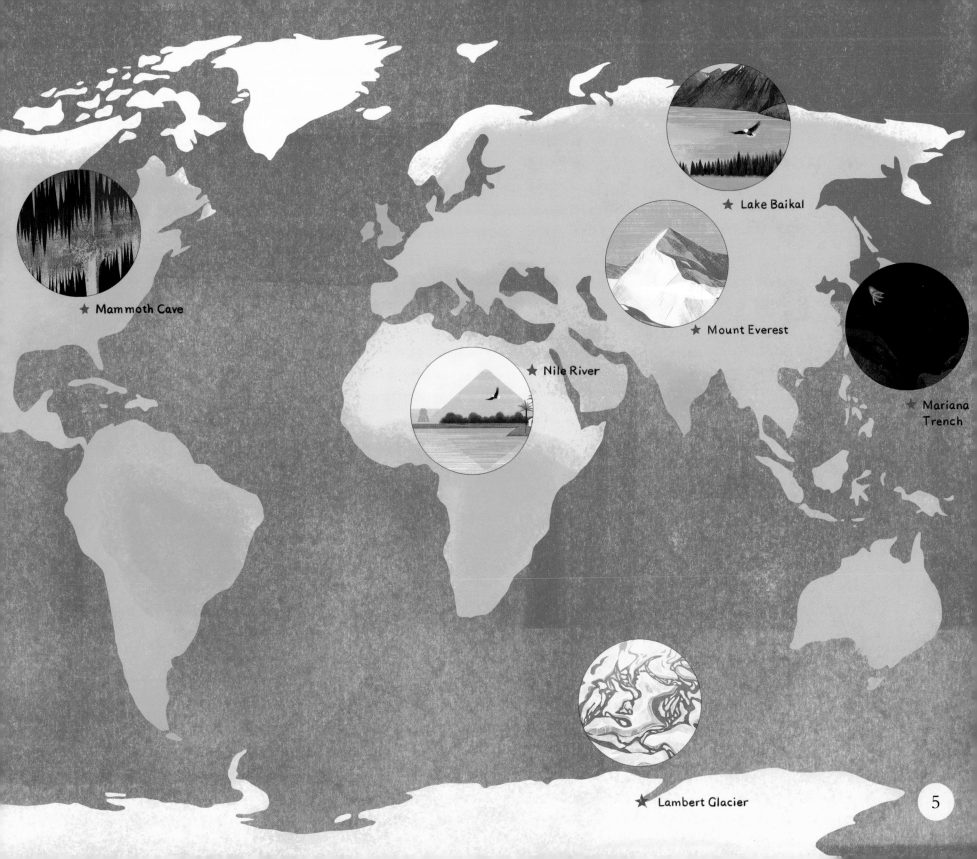

★ Lake Baikal

★ Mount Everest

★ Mammoth Cave

★ Nile River

Mariana
Trench

★ Lambert Glacier

5

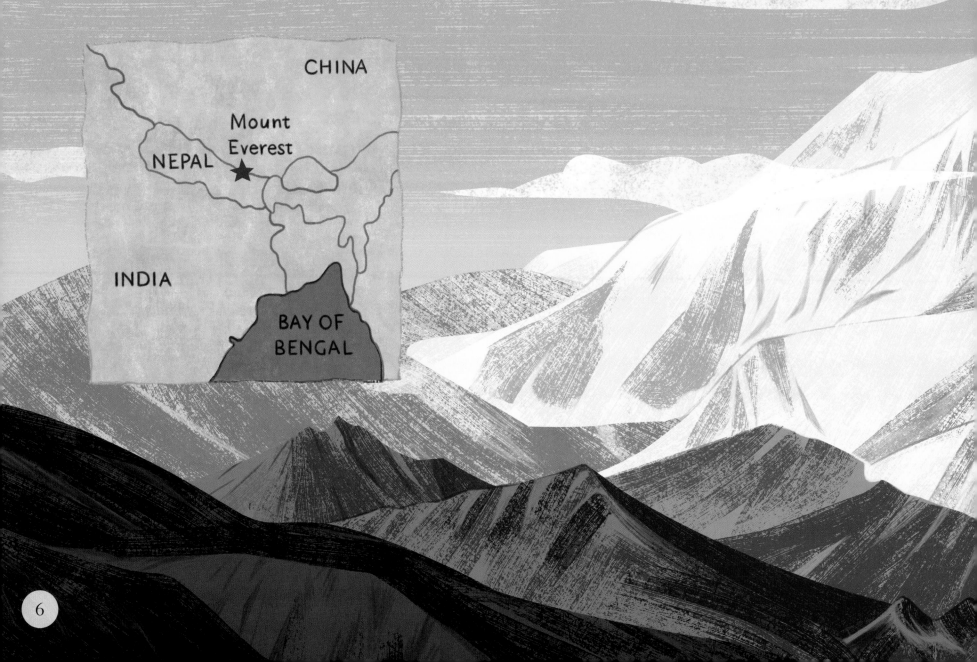

Mount Everest lies within Nepal.

Its snowy peak juts in the sky.

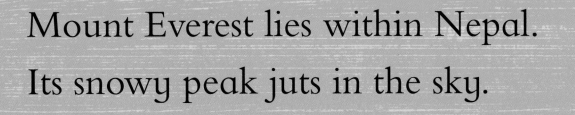

CHINA

Mount
Everest

NEPAL

INDIA

BAY OF
BENGAL

Mount Everest, Nepal and China

World's Highest Mountain

(Highest above sea level, but not tallest)

Dimensions: 29,029 feet (8,848 meters) high

The highest mountain of them all,
it goes as high as airplanes fly.

Earth explorers, come discover awesome places like none other.

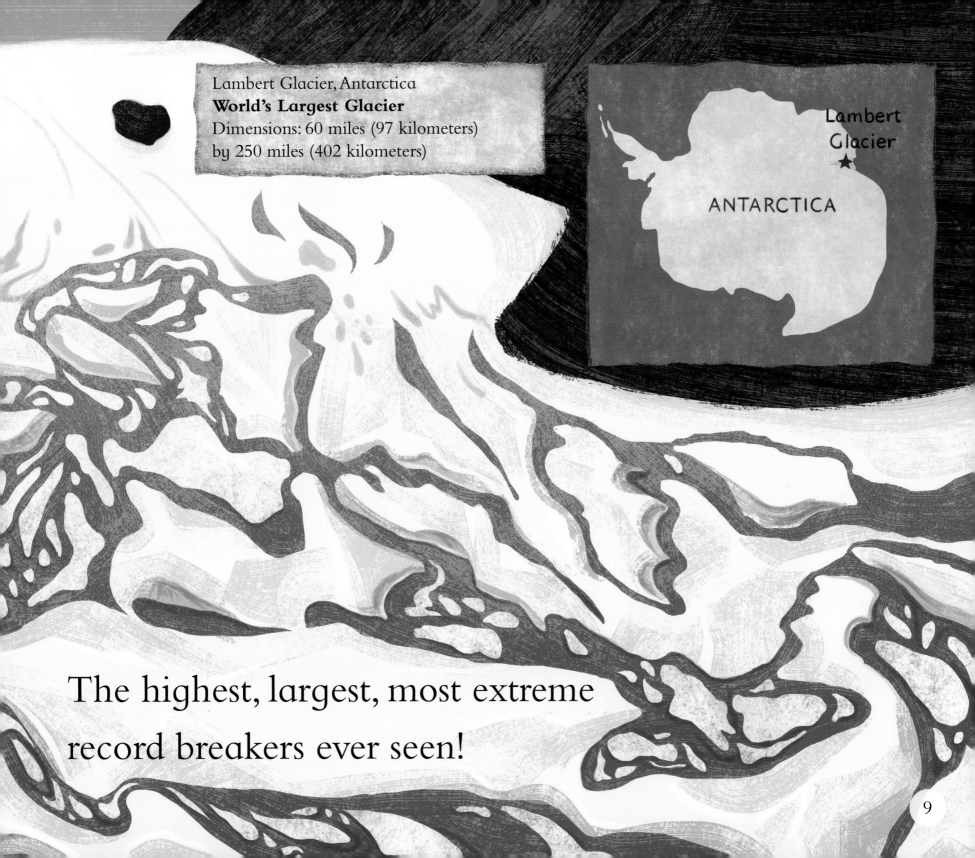

Lambert Glacier, Antarctica
World's Largest Glacier
Dimensions: 60 miles (97 kilometers)
by 250 miles (402 kilometers)

Lambert
Glacier

ANTARCTICA

The highest, largest, most extreme
record breakers ever seen!

The Pacific is the largest ocean.
It colors Earth a sparkling blue.

Pacific Ocean
World's Largest Body of Water
Dimensions: Covers about one-third of the globe

RUSSIA

CANADA

Pacific Ocean

Rhythmic waves in endless motion.

Five **continents** enjoy its view.

Earth explorers, come discover awesome places like none other.

Mariana Trench, Pacific Ocean
World's Deepest Spot
Dimensions: 36,070 feet (10,994 meters) deep

The highest, largest, most extreme
record breakers ever seen!

The most active volcano of all sits on the shores of Hawaii.

PACIFIC OCEAN

HAWAII

Kilauea

Kilauea Volcano, Hawaii
World's Most Active Volcano
Erupting every day since 1983
Pronounced "KILL–eh–WAY–uh"

Down Kilauea **lava** crawls,
year after year, down to the sea.

Earth explorers, come discover
awesome places like none other.

RUSSIA ★ Lake
Baikal

MONGOLIA

CHINA

Lake Baikal, Russia
Lake that Holds the Most Water
Dimensions: 5,387 feet (1,642 meters) deep

The highest, largest, most extreme record breakers ever seen!

In Africa, past desert sands
the longest river floods and flows.

EGYPT

★

Nile River

RED
SEA

The Nile River, Northeastern Africa
World's Longest River
Dimensions: 4,258 miles (6,853 kilometers) long

Past **pyramids** and **storied** lands
the mighty Nile River goes.

Earth explorers, come discover awesome places like none other.

The highest, largest, most extreme record breakers ever seen!

Mammoth Cave, Kentucky
World's Longest Cave System
Dimensions: 406 miles (652 kilometers) of passages

The highest, deepest, tallest, largest,
spewing-streams-of-lava-longest,
truly awesome, most extreme
record breakers ever seen!

SONG LYRICS
Earth's Record Breakers

Mount Everest lies within Nepal.
Its snowy peak juts in the sky.
The highest mountain of them all,
it goes as high as airplanes fly.

Earth explorers, come discover
awesome places like none other.
The highest, largest, most extreme
record breakers ever seen!

The Pacific is the largest ocean.
It colors Earth a sparkling blue.
Rhythmic waves in endless motion.
Five continents enjoy its view.

Earth explorers, come discover
awesome places like none other.
The highest, largest, most extreme
record breakers ever seen!

The most active volcano of all
sits on the shores of Hawaii.
Down Kilauea lava crawls,
year after year, down to the sea.

Earth explorers, come discover
awesome places like none other.
The highest, largest, most extreme
record breakers ever seen!

In Africa, past desert sands
the longest river floods and flows.
Past pyramids and storied lands
the mighty Nile River goes.

Earth explorers, come discover
awesome places like none other.
The highest, largest, most extreme
record breakers ever seen!

The highest, deepest, tallest, largest,
spewing-streams-of-lava-longest,
truly awesome, most extreme
record breakers ever seen!

Earth's Record Breakers

World
Mark Oblinger

Verse

1. Mount Ever-est lies with-in Ne - pal. Its snow-y peak juts in the sky. The high-est moun-tain of them all, it

goes as high as air-planes fly.

Chorus

Earth ex - plor - ers, come dis-cov - er awe-some plac - es like none oth - er. The high-est, larg-est, most ex -

treme re - cord break - ers ev - er seen! (skip to **Outro** last time)

Verse 2
The Pacific is the largest ocean.
It colors Earth a sparkling blue.
Rhythmic waves in endless motion.
Five continents enjoy its view.

Chorus

Verse 3
The most active volcano of all
sits on the shores of Hawaii.
Down Kilauea lava crawls,
year after year, down to the sea.

Chorus

Verse 4
In Africa, past desert sands
the longest river floods and flows.
Past pyramids and storied lands
the mighty Nile River goes.

Chorus

Outro

The high - est, deep - est, tall - est, larg - est, spew-ing - streams-of - la - va - long - est, tru - ly awe - some, most ex -

treme re - cord break - ers ev - er seen!

GLOSSARY

continents—the seven major bodies of land on Earth. From largest to smallest, they are Asia, Africa, North America, South America, Antarctica, Europe, and Australia.

extreme—very unusual

lava—hot, melted rock that flows out of volcanoes

pyramid—a pointed structure with sides shaped like triangles. Egypt's ancient pyramids are a famous sight.

storied—having an interesting or famous history

GUIDED READING ACTIVITIES

1. Share this song with friends and family. Can you find someone who has visited one of the places in this book?

2. Your own state has record breakers. Can you find some? What is your state's highest point? What is its largest body of water?

3. Of all the places in this song, which one would you like the visit most? Why? Draw a picture of yourself there.

TO LEARN MORE

Bellisario, Gina. *To Planet Earth!* Minneapolis: Millbrook Press, 2017.

Dickmann, Nancy. *Mount Everest*. Chicago: Raintree, 2013.

Simon, Seymour. *Seymour Simon's Extreme Earth Records*. San Francisco, CA: Chronicle Books, 2012.

Throp, Claire. *The Nile River*. Chicago: Raintree, 2013.